ISSUE 2 | EMBODIMENT | AUTUMN, 2023

CONTENTS

KITH REVIEW IS PUBLISHED BY CINNAMON PRESS
Office 49019
PO Box 15113
Birmingham
B2 2NJ
info@cinnamonpress.com

Editor: Jan Fortune
Design & Layout: Adam Craig.
Cover design uses photos by Leon Liu/Unsplash
(front cover) and Annie Spratt/Unsplash (back
cover)

ISBN 978-1-78864-806-6

Bonnie Thurston

Self Examination

What do you think, my sister,
when you touch your own breasts?

Whose fingers press your pink
or bronze or beautiful black flesh?

Are they sterile, technical fingers
compressing you in a cold machine?

Are they the lover's who knows
how to delight and ignite you?

Are they his who roughly took
and degraded your loveliness?

Are they the lips of your babes
which elicited such complex sensations?

For what do you search, my sister,
when you touch your own breasts?

Picasso Exhibit

Alongside they screened
an old, Italian film
of the master at work,
barely clad not to hinder
the body's movement,
the earth's own energy
he made manifest.

Comparing it to my limping
attempts at word craft,
stumbling, scratching revisions,
I was stunned by his fluidity,
assurance, speed, steadiness
of composition—totally
without pause or hesitancy.

I saw the conflagration
that burned in head and heart
meet at the shoulder,
run down the arm,
flow from the hand
that held the charcoal,
almost glowing crimson
when it touched the wall
with its dancing flame,
becoming a living female form.

It was as if his totems,
the dove (Aphrodite's
soul messenger)
and the owl (Athena's
messenger of death),
swooped a miraculous helix
of wisdom and peace.
When the figure was finished,
the film maker announced
workmen had thought her graffiti
and whitewashed the wall.
Divine fire cannot be quenched.
Someone will pick up charcoal,
and re-ignite the dance.

Old Tart

This time of year
my world spreads itself out
like a blowsy, old tart
whose customer has left
early in disgust.
She could care less,
drops tomatoes in profusion,
more than I can bottle
there have been so many.
I forget to pick runner beans
which grow fat, lazy, tough.
'We dare you to eat us all,'
they taunt and droop.
The flowers are bloomed out,
exude the perfume of decay.
The trees, fully leafed,
are no longer fresh, lush,
just profuse, plethoric.
It is all turgid, cloying.
I would be repelled
if I didn't know
the lonely, old tart
will soon roll languidly
over into the lusty arms
of winter and death. **KR**

Jan Fortune

in the forest is a world and the world is life

in the forest is a world and the world is life   above, below, root and branch, leaf and root, root and flower, as above, the flower nursing aeons, this atom of leaf that was atom of mollusc, this sliver of bark once cells of the hart's beating heart. *a leaf of grass is no less than the journey work of the stars.* listen. once upon all time, always upon every time, in the forest is a world and the world is life, and the forest is one and the world is one, and all is life and death, death a passage through life, as above, so below, decay to life, rotting to recycle, dissolution to rebuild, worm becoming toe of dog becoming fingernail of musician becoming petal of rose becoming root of oak becoming… a different story, this sapling oak containing *gneiss, coal, long-threaded moss, fruits, grains, esculent roots,* this moth that was shitake's body, *and mossy scabs of the worm fence, heap'd stones, elder, mullein and poke-weed* are the world, are the universe, are the forest and the forest is a world and the world is life. linger. the world is here, under and over, as above, so… the oak asks, *what is the grass?* flesh of earth's flesh, flesh of oak's flesh, flesh of all flesh, it is grass that was a different story, that died, was reborn, will be another story and… *the beautiful uncut hair of graves* come to life to die again, *and to die is different from what any one supposed, and luckier.* listen. in the forest is the story and the story is unwording into light, into waves, into fragments that are all things, light waving into words that are story of the forest that is world, that is a maze in a garden beneath the shadow of a mountain beside a river where salmon might swim and hedge of hawthorn and yew twist and turn, turn and twist, dead-ending, mischieving, gathering round the hazel of knowledge where the ground is prickly with yew and thorns… and yew whisperes the long view of ancestor becoming, death ceding to life   where forest is life, where forest sings light, where… listen to the story that is healing unworded, that grows in tree and herb, in mushroom and shrub, in berry and bud, healing pulsing light and death, dark and life, healing sweet as yew's scarlet aril, bitter as adieu. linger. in the forest is a world and the world is life and it calls… listen. linger. here is all that is green, all that is needful, all that has been and will ever be, here is the universe in a ripening bramble fruit, creation in the dew on a lady's mantle leaf, here is food and song, medicine and poison, here is the story of all that can ever be, wound in an acorn, patterned in a mugwort leaf, papered into birch bark, dappling in the dancing light, in the forest is a world and the world is life. **KR**

HELEN MAY WILLIAMS

metaphor in action

yellow
flag iris

Photos by Annie Spratt & Maury Lima on Unsplash

I'm going to tell you an anecdote of how I spent an autumn weekend three decades ago. I spent it on my knees in mud with my hands and forearms plunged in stagnant water. I was trying to clean the garden pond in order to encourage wildlife into my garden and to provide a habitat for frogs and toads, who even then had to rely on garden ponds since brooks and streams were being lost to development. I had dug the pond six years previously, when my children were still in primary school. Indeed, they and their friends helped me dig it.

However, half a dozen years had passed by, and it seemed time to remove some of the Yellow Flag Iris, to make more room for the frogs. You may not be familiar with Yellow Flag Iris; it reproduces through seeds which are born in long, fat pods, divided into compartments. Several seedpods on one stem. It also reproduces vegetatively by thick, fleshy rhizomes, which are immensely strong and spread under the surface of the water to produce a thick, woven mat of ripe, deep pink-brown firm flesh. If that were not enough, the rhizomes send out long, white, water roots, which appear as gently waving tendrils, but which tie themselves in knots with one another and prove as fast as any string I've ever come across. In addition, the rhizomes put out another kind of root, when they sense there is mud around which they can draw substantial nourishment from. These roots are dark grey, almost shiny, lizard-like, and undulating in texture. Clustered together it is difficult to know for sure if they are vegetable or animal in character. Rather than the roots of a plant, they resemble some new amphibious species, multiplying in close, thick communities.

I struggled with all this all Sunday afternoon, until the dark overtook me. As the working week began with the usual round of Monday lectures and seminars, I knew I had still to return to complete it. What struck me as I got muddier and muddier, watched live frogs escaping from the scene, and unearthed the occasional frog skeleton, was that these Flag Iris had managed to multiply, simultaneously in two different ways, but more than that: they had formed a complex living mat of differing root systems, which intertwined and intertangled indiscriminately both laterally and vertically. It would have taken far more strength than I possessed to eradicate it by force alone; and the teasing out of stem, rhizome and different types of root systems required much patience and a tolerance of muddy discomfort.

So why am I telling you this anecdote? Partly because it is a conscious parody of Thoreau's *Walden*, an unnatural natural philosophy. Partly because it alludes to the work of Deleuze and Guattari. Partly because I think it offers an appropriate metaphor for our relationship with literature, both as authors and as readers. We cannot satisfactorily use simple systems of thought to make sense of the world any more. Just as one might describe the Yellow Flag Iris using a binary system of thought, as a water plant which reproduces both sexually and asexually, but in doing so would not start to describe the complexity of this plant colony, so if we try to describe the experience we have in relating the world and the experience we have of reading in this world as if it were a simple matter of binary categories, we will grossly disregard the complexities we face. It would be nice to move beyond a state of informed bewilderment, but in doing so we should remember that literature in our world is a vast web of interconnecting materials, with far more diversity of forms than my simple Yellow Flag Iris, with their beautiful flower spikes in late spring, their tall strong stems, their narrow leaves, their rhizomes and two kinds of root systems. It is all relative, it is all intertwined, it is all complex.

The metaphor of the rhizome, however parochial it might appear, is in fact one way of conceptualising the asymmetrical and opportunistic ways in which literary cultures inhabit the world. Three decades on, I miss those Yellow Flag Iris; I am planning to add some to my newly established bog garden this spring. ᴋʀ

Hare crossing

A stand off in headlights
passage maker Moon observed
in its cold angles I know you see me
halted erect and foreleg lifted
like the weighing of nothing between musics
With that mystery of ears in the old motif
I don't quite get you
But I make this pact
at each conjunction and moon at full
to consider more strangely chance and crossings
in fluidity of forest and field
and marks in frost as true to memory
as negatives of hands on walls of caves
and read absence in the depth of furrows
your breath a dampness on the uncurling leaf
and every hedgerow a flowering into molten air
I drive on to streets of lockups and steel shutters
I need eggs and milk
Graffiti dazzles under the late store sign
A failing striplight makes screenshots of freezer glass
its web of prints our leavings
Once I saw an artist paint a hare
She wetted paper washed layer on layer
till form emerged like setting frost
and process framed a question
when round her outline she filled solid black
then layered it with gold leaf
Because, she explained, before it leapt,
base colours hold true
Then lit a moon to dazzle us

Mick Evans

The flight from The Beehive

which is cursive and laudable in the clear wake of dogs and trades
to van doors wide with downed wreckage of kitchens and scaffolding
trailer loads squeeze through their emporia exuding stink and importance
in the bar continuum of the widescreen hum over froth and lamentation
and the church windows' blue glasseyed holy damsels stay medieval
until wings on the river spell merit

on the table the computer hums for uncertainty
while love halts towards the hedgerows' gated ways of earth and air
lifting bronze history and lake myth into skylines
all this is wisdom and being and essence
dogs congregate in covens planning their dark business
primrose and hawthorn suckle us
and shades return full sun into *a tendency and a habit*
distilling natural gratitude in the old year's mead and cider
such are days

the procession of the flower seller and purveyors of flesh and bread
sing out their fragrances
and travellers go in quest of milk and honey
all this is home and poses what that is
knowing one's place and connected
like the talk when I pause to buy stamps
transactions in a hive of transformation that sweeten raw matter
into tenable forms of love
every day to set off to sharps of the blackbird crossing my path
knowing we're offbeat headstrong
for early madrigals and the viable lands

The waterfalls at Cwmsawdde bridge

Every day the river makes new offerings
Plastic flaps a fin the kingfisher a lightness
Snagged boughs shade kindness over minnows
and rocks upstart sweet diversions

questioning what will you make of us
How state the heron's unburdening into air
and the otter unseen still a promise
How prime these hills in the scale of their healing

When a friend palms the primary of a kite
red brown to the heart unearthly
the land teems rivulets towards a focus
Three hours down from the mountain is white water over falls

I said I have known it bitter with ice
heard that low conversation every day
made it this far to where it breaks its heart
but gathers and restores

and take these tender proofs of calm
the natural state to be self possessed
and tranquil in the assurance
that everything fades towards restoration

Here water cannot bear reflection
but trace the graffiti under the bridge
its sorrow its heartease of love's leavings
towards quiet pools of adamant stone **KR**

Sue Proffitt

The skeleton speaks

As I understand it
I have separated now

into parts: a constituency
of selves. There's nothing broken;

rather, it is a freeing –
all the sacking and glue

the warm music of the body
departed. Emptied out,

each segment once used,
once useful, lies quiet

says *look at me*.
I am architecture.

The scaffolding that gave you
coherence. The house you

inhabited. 'I never knew,
you might say, your beauty.'

Bird

Flotsam from a cat's paw
here between my breasts
on the bed

you rest
and I watch the sea,
feel us rise and fall,

how you approach, slowly,
your body again

from wherever white terror
vacated you,

clicking your beak softly.

Do you want to enter
this life again,
its traps and starvings?

Now, your tiny head
lifts, blinks, flicks
side to side.

Outside,
something sings
on the sill

but we wait
until light
springs you open –

        you decide—
        jump into yourself—

        fly.

Supermarket

At the checkout, you standing beyond the till,
me paying, I was still wet, still sticky,
still feeling your head's unkempt brush
nuzzling between my legs, our bed
only five minutes bare, warm with our smells,
my skin electric, ticking, as if you were still there
inside me—we stared at each other
and something feral jumped—
a hot bright breaking—
you hovered inches above my face,
saliva dropping from your bottom lip,
I smelt your hunger.
I could have lifted my throat to you then,
watched you grip it.

Jan Fortune

writing in touch

Why we need to be

BOTTLE

To live in hope, expectation and wonder, we need to be bodiful. It's so easy for those of us involved in creative tasks, especially writing, to become cerebral and sedentary. Yet great art and great writing demand connections to the body and to the world. Artists need to find ways to connect; not to cut ourselves off, not to imagine ourselves as disembodied minds. The urgency of the times we live in, both politically and ecologically, scream against this. We need to

- Breathe in and be aware of our bodies, ourselves.
- Become attuned to our body's blockages, discomforts, tensions.
- Walk and move in the world that feeds our senses, which in turn nurtures our imaginations.

1 The bodifulness of enworlded soul

We are not minds (subjects) looking at bodies as objects we lumber around in, but whole creatures, intelligent bodies that are not as separate from the world as contemporary individualism has suggested.

The question of where the individual mind-body complex ends and the rest of the world begins is one that has exercised philosophers for generations. Husserl asserted that the lived body is the centre of experience, whilst Merleau Ponty talked about it being not thought but the world that is the realm of experience in which everything we touch in turn touches us. We don't understand the world from the perspective of disembodied minds. Rather, the body is the primary vehicle of knowing. And mind is rooted not only in body but in the body's interactions with the world. Ultimately, distinctions between mind, body and world may be arbitrary.

Within this matrix, the self is an elusive thing. The moment we attempt to step outside of ourselves to observe we are objectifying a version of the self that is more likely to be someone else. Virginia Woolf puts it simply:

One can't write directly about the soul. Looked at, it vanishes.

In another diary entry she talks about 'the slipperiness of the soul' and about its delicacy and complexity.

Writers, creators, all of us, are enworlded, soulful bodies, imagining quests, writing the stories of our cultures and of the people we want to be, creating art that images how the world can become a different story—whether that art is sculpture, textile or a feast.

2 The bodifulness of emotion

If we fancy some strong emotion, and then try to subtract all the feelings of its characteristic bodily symptoms, we find we have nothing left behind, no "mind-stuff" out of which the emotion can be constituted. Only a cold and neutral state of intellectual perception remains.

The notion that cognition and emotion are embodied is not only rooted in the philosophy of thinkers like Martin Heidegger, Maurice Merleau-Ponty and John Dewey, but we also see it most simply in our use of metaphors. We talk about being 'up' as a metaphor for happiness or 'down' for sadness, for example. The physical, embodied directions become metaphors. Similarly, several metaphors originate in physical interactions from childhood, so that, for example, affection becomes synonymous with warmth.

Thought requires a body, not in the obvious sense, but in the sense that the structure of thought itself arises from the body. Nearly all of our metaphors are based on shared bodily experiences. In short, thinking is embodied. And if metaphor is fundamental to who we are as humans and if this in turn is embodied, it behoves artists to embody their work. Despite the seemingly disembodied state of flow when we are immersed in creating a novel or a painting, in fact we always remain bodies in

Photo by Nathan DeFiesta on Unsplash

Aut

context. We see this when we realise how easy it is to disrupt flow with interruptions or distractions. Rilke understands this perfectly in *Letters of Rainer Maria Rilke*: when he talks about how mind and blood are continuous with each other.

3 The bodifulness of connection

Our writing should take note of embodiment not only because we are bodies but because it is how we connect—to others, to animals, to plants, to the universe, to the seasons, to the winter when we are often pulled inward, or to the mid-point of the year when we feel the sap of creativity everywhere. We are intimately connected to everything and unless we wake up to this, as individual creators and as a species, we will run out of a planet on which to live and think and love and make. The substance of the stars and of our bodies is the same. We are linked to every other atom of the universe and we survive or perish with every other life.

We stand at a point in history when we either speak up for our embodiment and intimate connection to all that is alive, to all that is material, or we face extinction with it. If we are to be creative people who make a difference to the world's story, we need to feel ourselves part of all nature.

In *The Songs of Trees*, David George Haskell finds such connection wherever and whenever we take tentative steps to listen to all that is life; whenever we locate our ethics and authenticity in relationships; wherever we pay deep attention.

Writers, artists, makers of all kinds… cannot afford to be creatures of the mind only, labouring under an illusion of separateness. What we are about is not cerebral, remote, and of no consequence. No matter how smart technology becomes and no matter how f r a g m e n t e d modern life can feel, we never cease from being

creatures of sensations whose bodies have evolved in the context of our survival needs. When we forget this, we are less than human. We need to be in touch with air, with other life forms, with scent to be human at all.

4 The bodifulness of the Numinous

Being embodied, being participants in a new story of the world, has never been so urgent, yet daily life can sometimes leave us feeling as though we live a huge amount of time only in our heads, even though our minds don't simply perceive the world in a disembodied way. Of course, this sense of embodiment is not to decry a state of flow that can be experienced as other-worldly, mystical and touching on the Numinous, but it is a call to bring back what we find there and connect it to how we live. Being connected, being embodied, being in flow; experiencing the Numinous of nature or of the profound transcendence of writing are not dichotomies, but of a piece. Imagination begins in the senses and then takes us to new places of connection.

5 The bodifulness of time

This slippery soul that Virginia Woolf referred to, with its ever shifting and evolving elements is grounded in our bodily experience and also in our experience of time. To quote Woolf again:

> Consciousness is tied to corporeality and temporality: I experience myself as existing as a body over time. Humans live embodied in time. Time is how we make sense of concepts like 'self' and 'relationship'. It's how we remember the narrative of our life: the food we ate, the places we saw, the people we were with… It's how we plan our lives, by imagining forward to where we will be and what we will be doing.

Our embodied entwining with time is at the heart of identity in so much literature. Kafka was certain that:

> Reality is never and nowhere more accessible than in the immediate moment of one's own life.

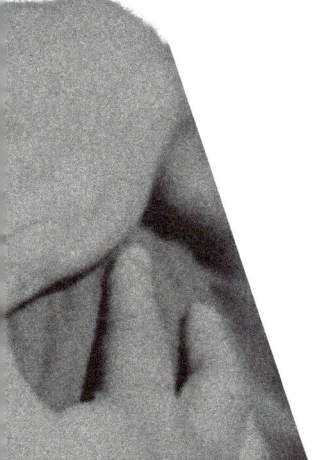

And filmmaker, Andrei Tarkovsky, says that we watch film because it gives us a sense of time.

Life often feels like a constant dance with time. I have periods when I'm convinced that 'there is no time' and others when it appears that time is boundless and I can fit in enormous amounts of activity or being. Finding rhythm and balance in this bodiful quest keeps alive memory and allows new stories to unfold. We do this by living, as far as life allows, in kairos time, not simply linear chronos, but the ripe moments of now. We need to live in ways that allow us to linger, listen and connect. We need to be in our bodies which embody soul, emotion, the numinous, the senses—all that we pour into our art. KR

John Sewell

A Pair of Swans

for Tess

Night. The Severn in full, midwinter flood.
Riverbank and garden five feet under,
the inundation a mere grassy slope
away now, from the French doors we peer through.
Has it topped the paving yet? Are the pair
of mated swans who sailed in here at dusk
between the tops of the hydrangea
(respite from the turmoil swirling south)
still with us, still becalmed?

                                  Yes, there they are.
Two ghost-moons float the water side by side.
Twin glimmers in the dark. Their necks and heads
in downy rest. Unconcerned
at what could happen next. The dawn will come,
of course it will. They'll be together.

Seeing the Special

Spring Equinox

Month after month
the remorseless river
swept us away
from all we held dear.

Then this bridge of skylarks
and these tiniest white flowers—
lark notes dropped to earth—
brightening the way.

We'd stepped on them
unknowingly, had no clue
what they were, or why
they shone so in their newness.

Or knew to be there, to prompt
your reached-out hand
as the song climbed on
exactly as it always had.

Shap Summit

For fifty minutes beside the line, a lark
was singing behind our words, our doing what we did
back in the day: your bike by the fence,
asking if the Pullman had gone through?

This excursion brought it back - our courting years
then marriage, kids, divorce. Yet here we were
essentially unchanged, the way it felt
to hear you say my name - with such excitement

when the 'Duchess' came, to re-acquaint us
with her rose maroon, her heart-stopping hundred tons
of quick-beat heat and thunder hurtling past,
lamplit tables at each carriage window, faces, lives,

the long climb gained, her loud exhaust-beat
drumming double at the overbridge -
then gone, in wreaths, then wisps of smoke.
And nothing left behind but lark song.   (cont.)

Gate of Light

Are they fighting or courting?
Flusters and tanglings
in tussock and heather.

Do skylarks pair for life?
I'd say we had, a thousand times over,
whether we go on to sing
or never speak again.

What comes alive
before that gate, takes centre stage
in all my dreams.
.

Never otherwise,
I swear.
First; last. Ends
of the earth. Beyond. **KR**

on bad days

now is a memory

ISABELLE LLASERA

L'Aubier

On bad days, she clams up. And as the thread that links words to things is so totally broken, it is as if she's been forced into exile in a foreign land filled with meaningless objects and strangers speaking incomprehensible tongues. At least that's where you imagine her to be. For what do you know? You too have to make do with what you have and devise a story. And some days, she just sits there, not here (where?), not responding to or acknowledging anyone's presence, eyes dark and glaring, darting right and left, body stiff, ready to pounce.

On one of those days, sitting in the lounge, you cast quick glances up at her then let your gaze linger over the photo on the back page of an old magazine on your lap. It shows an eerie inflated white silhouette heading towards a huge leaning black pylon in the background. It is disturbing and scary. It could have been taken on Mars or on an unknown planet. It takes a while before you realise the inflated silhouette is a model in a white billowing dress walking towards the Eiffel Tower. You didn't recognise the damn monument. You saw a robot, not a human being. And the photo, an advertisement for a fashion designer, scared and disturbed you. So this must be it, you tell yourself, this must be how the world appears to her, more and more often now, everything, even the most familiar, distorted, topsy turvy, absurd, forbidding and unstable, with floors slipping perhaps, lights dimming, pillars leaning and strangers throwing in weird sounds as they pass by. Where can she be then, when she sits frowning, hands gripping her handbag over her stomach, but alone, inside an alien, hostile, terrifying land, trapped inside her body, inside a web of sensations, chained to the present and entangled in a string of disconnected moments?

A moment. Then another. Going, going, gone. One after another. Now here. In the blink of an eye, not here. Then the next one. There and pfftt. Zooms off. Is gone. Then another. There. Not there. Quick as lightning. Whizzes off. Run as fast as you can, run, run, you won't ever catch it, won't ever bring it back, can't ever repeat it. It's over. Over and done with. In one minute flat. Gone off. Gone like a bullet. Forever over. Each one gone. In an instant. Gone.

A moment does not last longer than itself and forever and ever, succeeds to another. But that's according to the ticking of the clock. Tick, tock, tick, here, tock, gone.

If it wasn't for the memory of them, life would be just that, tick, tock, tick, tock, a succession of moments that go as they come.

They appear in all shapes those memories that break the inexorable mechanics of the clock. At times, they might be driftwood planed down by currents, brought in by tides on the seashore, driftwood we pick up and whittle out, fill in, carve and join to other carved moments to turn them into stories so that they will endure and we can share them. At others, they're porous stones we keep inside a walled garden we visit when we please, stones we lift to find what swarms and grows beneath. Or they drop inside a vessel we carry with us, a vessel we can turn to and tilt to let them trickle out or flow when it's too cold and we're alone, or when the world around us narrows and the horizon shrinks and all we see ahead is fog so that, as they ooze out or gush, we may live periods of the past again.

They make up the malleable and fluctuating stories of our lives and like clouds in the wind, they morph and now and then, patterns may appear and sense emerge as we linger over them, sort out, discard or add, shape and share and reshape. But with time, we lose the strength to pick up pieces of wood to carve or lift stones and on the vessel, a tiny crack appears, and then another and it begins to leak and memories seep out then spill, and as the cracks widen, the flow won't stop and the vessel empties and, as time carries on with its relentless work, it scrapes its sides and hollows it out till all that is left is mud at the bottom.

Perhaps the dregs, buried deep inside the mud where no words can be heard or uttered, are what your mother kept quiet about and wanted to forget, what she turned her back on when she left to go to England after the war. Perhaps it is inside the muck at the bottom of the vessel that her stubborn, bossy ghosts live on and, now that all the rest has spilled, they feel they own the place and go on a rampage when they want.

So that the only memories she's left with are those that were never stitched together, never made it to story form, those that seem to come from nowhere, uninvited, rough and raw, responses to a sting, a breeze, a blow, a blast that, in forgotten circumstances, stabbed or soothed or slapped and whacked and scared, and now, because she hears a groan or touches fur or sees an exhausted crowd, or because her hair is being combed, they're back, and hit or prick or soothe or slap, and scare all over again.

When your mother sees the throng of wheelchairs trying to board the lift, she isn't only reminded of her attempts at reaching safety with three Jewish children, she's actually back there, gripped by the fear she felt as, seventy years earlier, they struggled to board overcrowded trains and flee. When she buries her face in the fur of the nylon coat you bought her, she's immediately filled with the teenage joy she felt when her father gave her her first fur coat. When an auxiliary comes to give her hair a trim, like a flayed animal, like the sheared women she saw but can't recall, she's terrified. And when she hears the cries and moans and groans of other residents, she doesn't recollect those of the tortured prisoners down the lane where she lived but, as if the decades between now and then had been abolished, the horror that seized her at the time whams back at her and she's as exposed as a palimpsest, the multiple imprinted layers of her life having been scraped, erased, torn out. Time's thing, time's toy, she has no control over this, no say in it.

Is this it? Is this what accounts for her anxiety, her fears? Is this what leads her to despair, and so many others in l'Aubier judging by the vacant stares, the pleading gazes, the moans and cries, a despair which, in turn, leads to dementia. Their stories lost, their bodies shackled to present sensations, our elders are prey perhaps, to the dementia of despair.

'Do you think I ought to start thinking about a care home?' you'd asked your mother's GP one day.

'Yes,' she said, 'I think you should. But it'll be difficult. It's easier for women who've never worked outside their homes, or who had jobs as secretaries for instance, or whose husbands have always taken all the important decisions. It's easier for those who've been submissive all their lives. It'll be hard for your mother.'

A couple of years later, when it was time to start packing to move to l'Aubier, your mother went on a word and hunger strike of sorts. For two weeks she refused to speak or eat. You opened her wardrobe and chest of drawers.

'Shall I pack this jumper?'

'I couldn't care less,' she said.

'Would you like to take this dress?'

'It's all the same to me.'

'How about these photos?'

'Do as you like.'

'Would you like some soup tonight? Mashed potatoes? An egg?'

'I'm not hungry.'

Then she shrugged or shook her head in answer to your questions and clammed up completely. No food in, no words out. Her life, that semblance of a life, didn't concern her anymore. You forced a few tiny spoonfuls inside her mouth, packed her best clothes and a few old garments, her toilet case, a few pictures, photos, books and bits and pieces, and she moved to l'Aubier.

The entry in her big diary for the day she left her home is, *'I must be gone and live or stay and die' (Romeo and Juliet Act 3 sc 5).*

I'll throw myself out of the window if it goes on, your mother said. Throughout her life. Not often. When things went really wrong, when she couldn't face it, things going wrong, when she couldn't cope, when there was too much pain. Said it, mind you, never, as far as you know, attempted anything.

It's pain that made and makes her want to die. But pain comes and sometimes goes with drugs and when it eases, her love of life takes over. Even now, even in l'Aubier, she clings to the world by her failing hearing when there's music in the air, by her taste buds when she smells whiffs of juicy roast or creamy cake, by her weakening eyesight when she sees colours, movement, light.

Before her move to l'Aubier, shortly after her ninetieth birthday, in the first days of spring, she went down to her little blue car and found the battery flat after months of not having run during a long cold winter when she'd had bronchitis.

She called the nearby garage and asked them to come and recharge the battery.

I'm going to drive along the coast tomorrow, she told you over the phone one night when the car was ready. No, you're not, not tomorrow, you said. Why not? she asked. Wait till I come, you said. Wait? But I want to drive along the coast now, she said, weather's perfect. Look, we'll go together when I come, I'll be there in just a fortnight, you insisted. I really don't see why I should wait a fortnight, sun's out and warm, I'll drive to A, maybe stop for a coffee on the way and be back before the sun's down, that's all.

You knew that if she'd made her mind up, nothing you said would change it, that she was there already, in anticipation of it all, the first glimpse of the creek just after the bend and of the gnarled pines on the red rocks and, a little further, of the blue and gold shimmers between the tall dark pines along the wide beach, and the idea emerging for a charcoal or a pastel, and then the road signs pointing to Italy, and the plans forming to push there, as she sometimes did, for a plate of pasta with a glass of chianti and the music of the Italian tongue in her ears. But you also knew how she drove now, how she crawled along in first gear, moved into second gear only when the hooting behind became too loud, and said, what on earth is the matter with them, then played a cassette or switched the radio on and hardly ever looked in the rearview mirror or signalled when she turned.

Her neighbours told you she often hobbled down with her walking stick, sat in her car, started and was off. How long does she go off for? you asked. Oh, not sure exactly, they said, but, yes, a whole day sometimes.

After lunch, on leaving l'Aubier to go out on one of your little excursions along the coast and a cup of coffee on the seafront, she always asks, which car shall we take, mine or yours? You'd sold her car shortly after she moved to l'Aubier and tell her so each time. Oh, she says, you never told me, so I can't leave, I'm a prisoner now.

It took a long time to clear out her little blue car before you sold it. It was her second home, as crammed as a tiny house, but even better than a house, as it followed her whims and went where they took her. You found all sorts in it, a thermos, a small half empty flask of whiskey and plastic cups, a torch and boxes of matches, a sewing kit and a tin box with biscuits, sugar lumps and sweets, a note book and a sketch book, a box of pastels and charcoals, pencils and dried out felt pens, a jam jar with bandages and safety pins, a lipstick and a half empty bottle of eau de cologne, a poetry anthology, a few battered paper backs, old newspapers and art magazines, an old pair of leather gloves, a moth-eaten blanket, a flattened out cushion and a towel, a frayed silk scarf and a woollen one, a broken umbrella, a rain hat and an old jumper, a pair of worn out boots and plimsolls with socks stuffed inside them. Except for a bed, she had all she needed in her little blue car.

Shall I drive? she always asks when you get to your car to go for the ride to the seafront. Next time, you say. Oh, all right then, she sighs.

And if the mistral has cleared the sky of clouds and drugs have put her aches at rest, as she catches sight of the blue and gold glimmers between the dark parasol pines, winter or summer alike, she'll say, I shall have to look for my swimsuit soon.

It is as if the curved limbs swaying in the breeze were arms leading her down the path to the sand and to the soft flapping of the water, as if the light flowing over and out of the waves summoned her, as if the slow, deep, constant breathing of the sea lulled her back to beginnings, to past charmed moments that were beginnings, so that all the rest is gone, the fog ahead, lifted, the pains, the fear, the load of years, forgotten.

Oh, does she 'rage, rage against the dying of the light' when her pains ease.

Summer will soon be here, I must look for my swimsuit, she says, just a few weeks before she dies as we drive along the winding road on the Esterel coast and, after the bend, a ray of sun shows the way down the red rocky path, down to the creek, down to the gnarled pines leaning into the wind towards the sea.

La mer, la mer, toujours recommencée, you say.

Le vent se lève, il faut tenter de vivre! she says.

Were those moments worth it?

Weren't those moments worth it? **KR**

Kate Gough

Alive

my favourite time of year is Autumn — not for the leaves
{undulating flames} but for the Air: electric,
crackling with the negative charge of storms to come
until my lazy lungs *open* and my body *hums*.

i love it for the incomparable clarity of breath
~ [empty], and the tingle in my skin that births
Anticipation —
then
Awareness…

the air changes, and i feel it in my bones as
stiff leaves rustle and
hiss out of the trees, as the wind
trails across my face, cleansingly
full of sparks.

Everything speaks danger and ending now,
while life Endures,
)hidden(.

i dream of rosehip tea

it was months ago when i picked rosehips along my path home by the sea, slipping each one like a little gold nugget into the pockets of my grey, zip-up jumper. i'd imagined doing it so many, many times, like a child in a candy shop, reaching up to pluck the beauties down; this time, the temptation was too great, and i just gave in. 'jumpers wash,' i reasoned with my other, more fastidious self. 'and it is never too late to achieve a dream.'

it was so easy, so natural, smiling ivories to no one but my self as i stashed treasure after treasure. i just couldn't stop. i arrived home, pricked full of holes, thorny leaves poking carelessly out of my jumper (now folded carefully like a giant bag), hands full of whispery grass stems, lavender, and wildflowers, my heart breathless from *breathing* in so much all at once. 'i must do that again,' i told myself with the immovable, patient force of glaciers moving downhill. 'i must empty myself of the care that keeps me from breathing.'

i set them in a small, hand turned pot, enjoying how they looked while i found a suitable jar to be my wildflower vase and filled it with motive liquid crystal. i crushed a handful of those passionately red rosehips with mortar and pestle and poured them, ivory seeds peeking out of their thin skins, into a glass teapot, watching them soften in the steamy, boiling clarity, opening up to embrace my insides with a foreknowledge of their return to the earth. carelessly, i crushed a bit of cinnamon to fractious bark and added it to the pot.

'i don't know how to do this,' i said to the darkness in me. 'but i am joyous and fascinated all the same.' (the darkness made a little nest in the corner and watched me grumpily, brows squinched together.)

that night i slept like a baby, and woke up clear, full of light.

:Kyrie:

leaves
rustle
as lady wind stirs up
the souls of the trees.
it is early in the morning and
i am cutting carrots and cucumbers
at the sink.

all day yesterday it rained;
the cold, fresh air c r a c k l e d
with newness, and we breathed it in
like children
eagerly inhaling candies.

the trees outside speak to one another now
in low voices, and
i stop cutting vegetables,
going to the window in the pale light to
l i s t e n, begging them
to share their secrets
with me.

reaching out in the darkness
i hear them sigh, and
s h r u g, their massive joints creaking
wearily — or with sympathy;
i cannot tell.
the white tail of a rabbit
scampers away into the bushes and the
lady lifts the trees' leaves,
waving goodbye ~
{where on earth can we turn now for
c o m p a n i o n s h i p
but ourselves?
the human race has
outwitted itself:
grown old, weak and
self-absorbed.
we no longer know how to
l i s t e n
to any language
but our own.

Pores

The world gets into our pores
and writes on us

lines with the clay of
earth, warmth of sun
bite of wind caress;

sorrow & joy clog our faces
with our insides, the experience of
our lived Grund:connected.

Existentially, we are slow-born sculptures
that tell of a daring hand
a fiery eye, laced with Power and Love

Why hide it?
you can tell a lot by the face of a man
who hasn't washed it all away.

... That Thing With Wings

Autumn breathes on my face
from afar — so fresh! — stirring
every unique nerve ending to
sudden, electric life.

As if my mother's cool hand
rests gently on my arm,
I'm startled awake.

And out from the ashes of languid,
summer days, my heart rises
up and up, spiralling higher, higher,
higher still, feathered and beating in
deep reds and flashing golds,

inexplicably
Singing. **KR**

Kate Noakes

Your unfurled lungs are the size of a cricket pitch

This is a lie. While the hale and hearty
enjoy the unseason—a warm autumn day—
I hunker from the sun in my sick space, popping

anti-biotics as if they were sweets,
and resting to make something of the evening.

The cough of life's unfair hand hacks
at my chest like the thwack of ball on willow.

New lungs, please. Or, at least, a pair
not filled with the first sniff of September
not to empty until March.

Decant me, so I can do the things
others consider normal. Like, breathing.

For ailments of the lungs

His diary mentions coughwort
for the ailments of the lungs and I am all
wonder at a new plant. With British flora
I claim expertise and a school prize,
reward for my efforts with flower names,
but coughwort defeats me.

A tea might be worth the drinking,
if I can find the plant.
You might know it as ass's foot,
bull's foot, foal's foot, horsefoot.
The mystery is solved with coltsfoot,
a common place.

Its yellow daisies star the shingle
as far as the eye and flints allow,
constellations escape from Derek's
brilliant garden to glow across
the ochre, white and grey,
the stony sea of Dungeness.

They're the same custard shade
as the windowsills and doorframes
of Prospect Cottage, a-shimmer
against tarred clapboards.
Though they'd not have stopped
the TB ravaging his gut,
they might dry my lungs
in the salt wind of late summer. **ꓘꓤ**

For Echo

Reflections from a Practicing Poet

At a reading a few months ago, I stumbled on (and through) a phrase, in answer to a question from the attending audience, that for a brief moment stunned me into self-made silence. What I had found myself saying stopped me in my tracks. It was as if in articulating the thought in question I had managed to capture what writing poetry and, I suppose, what writing *tout court*, just *was* for me. I found myself (in the midst, as I say, of finding my self) saying that when I wrote a successful poem, a poem that was not just busy work, but perhaps the 'real thing', I was writing not as myself but as the person '*who I'd like to be*'. This small searing insight, this deft, intervening thought, had even more impact to my mind, in so far as I am, predominantly a lyrical poet, and a confessional one, most of the time, too. So, I was saying, in effect, that, for all my affecting authenticity or sincerity, or that which I tried to drum-up in writing then reading my verse, writing my verse to be read—my efforts were sourced in a *trajectory*; that the originating moment of my own creative activity was a kind of reaching-forth: for a personal utopia; it seemed that what I was always trying to make possible or indeed actual was something actually, in the strictest sense, impossible—or at least, impossible to completely achieve. And for a few days after I'd uttered this surprising but somehow strangely relieving notion, I thought on it. And I realised I'd hit on a truth that spanned all my creative efforts: writing for me was a way of projecting a persona, sure, was a performance, yes, that too, but more than these staple notions common to most writerly types: it was and is a way of bettering myself, if discretely or intransitively. But then the supplementary or complementary thought occurred that it wasn't just this; writing for me was a way for me to better myself in the eyes of others, and only thus, via redirect, in *my own* eyes. One's desire is always the desire of the other, or of the other's desire: this is perhaps one of Jacques Lacan's most homely truths, and it suits me down to the bone—even if the marrow protests, or protests too much. I'd like to be as baring and honest and nude here as possible, in these cursory reflections on my practice of writing.

Let me start by saying that I've noticed how in writing, whether in critical mode or in verse (but more implicitly in verse), I tend to lend myself authority. I'm a relatively erudite person, in anglophone literature (pound for pound of course), but like many a 'brilliant' type, the celerity of my mind, coupled with a certain childish ebullience and effusiveness, often make me 'over-reach'. It's as if I'm saying (and to myself first or most of all): 'well, I *could* really have earned the weight of that slightly pretentious judgment I've just aired, if I'd troubled to make the effort: so, it's the same thing in the end!' And the truth *actually is* that any meretriciousness I evince *really is* just a lack of time and effort spent in order to have earned whatever over-reaching notion I may have just penned. But that's still no excuse. However, when I say that I tend to lend myself 'authority', I don't actually mean that I'm being pretentious; it's a bit more subtle than that. To reprise a Lacanian notion, I think I tend to lend myself just a tidbit more authority than I really do possess in earnest, because I haven't ever truly 'traversed my imago'. This in effect means that in some pertaining sense, my psychology has stayed childlike in its dependency, that I haven't surpassed those authoritative figures (of any gender, in truth) and become autonomous, my 'own man'. And thus, whether in sweeping critical rhetoric, or, perhaps in something as simple as Capitalising the first initial of my lines of verse, I am in effect compensating for something missing, something missing that can only show its truly 'missing' face via a present or

All photos by Brandon Hoogenboom on Unsplash

positive token or rune. Writing, even the best writing one does, can often still be a screen; *but not a smokescreen*—one hopes, at least! Perhaps I'm being too honest, or modest. Perhaps I'm not.

So. Who is this person I want to be? Who is it, that is, my writing strides forth to (try to) make me be? I suppose the person I see in my more serious-minded verse (and in other kinds of writing too) is someone who is far from complacent, but who is resigned: at-one with himself, at-one with any circumstance— whether it's the former that directs the latter, or vice versa. A man of ultimate repose. Some of what I consider my best work is written, if you like, at the moment of (metaphorical) sunset, at the cusp of dusk, when the proverbial Owl of Minerva starts her flight. I am always looking-on, 'reflecting'. Perhaps the covert side of ambition and 'chasing time' (which is a behavioural tic in me) is a place in the mind's perspective that is always looking over the shoulder of one's passed life? Perhaps a raucous desirousness finds its twin and tonic in a kind of 'death instinct'—to invoke a Freudian conceit? And in my poetry, and at my best, this effect that may perhaps come-across, this tonal serenity, is I hope something more than mere nostalgia, more than just nostalgia. It might be construed, rather, as a kind of (metaphysical) justice.

Nostalgia is often seen, especially in today's twenty-first century's cultural climate, as too conservative, as defunct, as absent-minded and a-politicised. And perhaps to be nostalgic is indeed a tad unhealthy, because unrealistic, and thus, too, can be unsatisfying to a sensitised eye at an aesthetic level. So, even when I find myself busied with my cello or my organ-tones, I must hope that looking-back at things, whether the passage of decades or of

a moment, is more than just an unrealisable or fanciful effort. In fact, it's p r e c i s e l y because in the most obvious and literal sense time moves mercilessly in one linear d i r e c t i o n , progressively cutting the ground from under our feet as we age, that creative work, like writing, is or can be a way of reinvigorating the past, giving new life in more than one direction or dimension to what might otherwise be seen as just dead, passed things. The past, for a creative mindset, that is to say, can be an opportunity for the future. Or put it this way, if you like: just as if there is a God, a Person or Mind in which and for which all of time and temporal happening is immediately or immanently resumed in one still moment, so, perhaps for us *infinitely smaller* creators, when we write the truth (whatever that is) we are in a way touching or sharing in God-hood—what T.S. Eliot famously encapsulated in the phrase, 'the still point of the turning world'.

But, in wondering along like this, I've been wandering. I want to return to the 'person who I'd like to be', the person dramatised into shadowy being when I write my best work. And for this I'd like to ponder a while on the theme or mythos of narcissism. Truth be told to the best of my ability I don't actually know, beyond an obvious surface level, whether I am indeed narcissistic. Yes, when I have work, poetry or prose, published and thus reflected back to me; when the achievement or accomplishment proves like a mirror, shoring me up, permitting me to pat myself on the back, allowing me to feel 'worthy', 'validated', I am certainly an avatar or epigone of that fated chap, Narcissus. But I suppose, the 'person who I'd like to be', is one who doesn't in effect commit suicide (if inadvertently) for having been too prideful or conceited or fastidious. The person

I'd like to be is probably a man who gives 'Echo' back her flesh, filler for the hollows; the man, if you like, who rises from perusing and admiring himself, and sweeps Echo off her feet, embraces her, and makes love to her. That man is not me, as I say: but he just might be who I'm trying to be when I write at my best. And how—to prolong this extended metaphor—might one truly return Echo to herself? Certainly not by ignoring her, or even, better, writing of and to her from a distance, sidelong. I suppose the only way Narcissus can truly consummate himself into his better, alternate, counterfactual life might be merely to love her, Echo, *not write of or to her.* So, maybe the man I want to be via my best work, is a poet whose poetry writes itself back into silence. The truly happy man, I've always believed, is the man who doesn't need to express himself, or at least, not beyond his needs. The truly happy man doesn't write poetry or brilliant critical essays. He gets on with his day in daylight, working productively and without taking undue pride in the same, and by night, when he returns to his love, just loves her. This might be in fact an apposite image of justice. Not a line of verse nor the herald of a biting insight can ever equal the full repose of a happy man.

I surmise, thus, that when I write my 'real things', I must be trying to achieve more than self-satisfaction: it must be me trying to get to the other side of the mirror, the truer other side; to a different land, where a man can be happy; to a land that certainly doesn't *prohibit* the use of mirrors—because such a puritanical extreme would be merely another kind of libertinism by way of its dichotomous opposite; to a land where each man, like myself, uses a mirror to shave in the morning, perhaps to brush his hair—before he goes off to his day in daylight, waddling or striding, and thinking no more of mirrors. **NR**

Jan Villarrubia

Heliopsis

Your patient glance away from the camera
settles on the prairie you love, thick with sage and bunchgrass,
yellow stonecrop in crevices.
The heliopsis you planted by the shed a decade ago
comes up wild every spring.

Summer days like this with no wind, you stay outside for hours,
hang clothes to dry, pinch off faded sweet peas—
green stains your thumbnails even after scrubbing.
You watch for that one coyote to pass—
she looks over at you quick keeps going looks runs.
Douglas firs on the hills filter the rest of the world,
and on your land, the utility pole rises like a cross.

You are a whisper through the screen door,
your arms full of flowers.
In the kitchen you arrange
the blossoms in a coffee pot filled with water,
glide into his room, place the arrangement on the dresser.
You bend over the bed to kiss the eyelids of your only son, 46 today,
wipe the saliva trickling from his open mouth,
turn his frail body one-fourth around,
adjust his head on the pillow, brush his hair with your fingers,
sit at his side,
sing.

Sisters

Just the three of us, like the three graces or three fates or both.
A trinity, a completeness,
that summer afternoon in the country.
We nibbled on biscuits, cheese, strawberries,
filled ourselves with chocolate,
red wine shared with bees.
Itching with ant bites and heat, Katharine
pulled off her sun hat and gloves, dared
us to jump in the creek. We unlaced our shoes,

tossed them in the grass,
held our skirts up high, grabbed hands, and
tiptoed into the cold, golden water.
Marie plops down, pulls us both in with her.
Laughing, we relent and sit,
skirts and petticoats drift around us like
puffy lily pads, pink, yellow, blue.
Great splashing and dunking:
O! St. John! Are you here with locusts and wild honey?

We are baptised again!
In nomine Patris et Filii et Spiritius Sancti
Heavy with soaked garments,
we lie back, let the water hold us.
Head, hair, arms rest, float.
It is past, present, future.
We are one with the body of water,
with each other.
We are cleansed. KR

Yvonne Baker

I would like to be as water

Not a surge of swell and swirl
flooding all in its path
but a ripple of thin light
rising slowly to lap the walls
with the slip and slop of gentle waves
that lift books off the shelves
embrace once secure chairs
I'll flow and be one
with the shape of the room
and whether I touch
light on the window allowing
its warmth to seep through me
or trickle into the unknown crevices
of the sofa and the secret grime
between springs
everything will be delight
so that when it's time to subside
I'll trust the emptiness
untroubled by the smell of silt
mingled with brine
content that all I leave
on the walls are water-stains.

the sky is breaking

it trickles quietly almost
unnoticed

       patters
       splashes
       down
       splishing
splosh-stalled unable to sink

       a petrichor whiff
                 drifts
on damp air

       drops grow
       heavy
       heavier
wash-murmer the parched earth
            purling
trickle-gush
       into dry earth
with a satisfied gurgle-flow

water-flowers weep for joy **ᴋʀ**

the detail is in the story

Hawthorn

Susan Elsley

CRATAEGUS MONOGYNA

ENGLISH: MAY-TREE
SCOTS: BOOJANS, CHAW, HAW
GAELIC: SGITHEACH

Hawthorns can grow to ten metres as a tree and are often used as hedging. The early leaves can be eaten, and the autumn haws used in a jelly. In the past, it was thought unlucky to have hawthorn in the house, because the smell was associated with death. In some places, like the north of Scotland, hawthorns were regarded as trees of healing and were, and still are, hung with 'cloots' or cloths.

Sixteen million trees went down that night. The pines that had been planted in straight lines crashed through the understory slamming into moss, grass and rock. The branches of hollowed-out oaks cracked and split. The hawthorns at the edge of the park hardly bent in the wind.

Sheila-Ann hadn't slept again, feeling the weight of night press on her body. She'd got up at three and made a cup of tea, adding a slug of whisky to numb her wakefulness and to remind herself that she wasn't going to ask for sleeping pills. The wind whirled around the outside of the house, slipping through the gap in the window so she felt the air vibrate with its coolness.

The wind dropped by dawn, and she slept again. She only climbed out of bed when Bloom scratched at the front door for his morning walk. With his wiry body, and squint eyes, he was not as appealing as the other dogs on the park circuit, but he met all comers with an air of courtesy. Like Joe had.

Her sister had told her to get a grip.

'Everyone our age loses people,' Marie had said when they met for their weekly lunch. 'Make your peace with it, for god's sake.'

She'd let her sister chatter on and picked at her pasta. Joe had given her energy that helped her deal with the everyday in a way that had been impossible before. In their ten years together, she had learnt to paddleboard, climb mountains and had travelled to the edge of the Artic circle. All on their paltry pensions, and without giving a fig for what anyone thought. Maybe that was why she'd stopped trying, until Bloom pulled at her trousers and dragged her out.

She crossed the footbridge and opened the gate. One of the Scots pines had come down across the top path, so she turned left towards the hawthorns. In spring, the trees sent up their flowers, and the birds flocked. At this time of year, the hawthorns were clusters of wizened, gnarled boughs that looked as if they might not get through the winter.

When she reached the stream, there was a boy with a beanie and a long stick standing in front of the hawthorns. Bloom ran towards the boy, who turned and then looked back at the trees, but not before Sheila-Ann saw that he was crying.

She hesitated. If it had been her, she would have wanted a stranger to walk on and leave her alone. Let her weep by herself like she did at least once a day. She clenched her fingers, letting her nails stab her palms as a reprimand. She was a seventy-year-old woman. This was a child, no more than twelve or thirteen. She wiggled her shoulders like Joe had taught her, so she felt more confident and carried on walking. Bloom stood next to the boy, who put his hand down, as if deciding whether to pat the dog or push him away.

'He doesn't bite,' she called out.

The boy knelt and stroked Bloom, who licked his hands. He didn't hide that he had been crying. That was the benefit of a dog like Bloom, thought Sheila-Ann. He made the difficult seem everyday.

The boy pointed upwards. 'They're tangled. I don't know what to do.'

She looked up at the tree. The hawthorn was the backdrop to her daily walk, so she'd forgotten about the shoes which hung by their laces from the branches. Today, the shoes had been twisted by the wind, so they didn't hang neatly down anymore.

'I spent hours sorting them last week,' the boy said. He wiped his face with the back of his sleeve and scrunched up his eyes to blink away the wetness.

She moved closer to the tree and stood on her toes, to see if she could reach the first pair of trainers. They were about the same size as Joe's old boots which still sat in the hall.

'Those are my dad's,' said the boy. 'He gave them to me when I'd hung my new trainers here, because shoes in trees bring luck.'

'Good idea,' she said, wondering why she found it so hard to talk to other people, when the words seem to come so easily to everyone else. She grabbed the heel of the shoe, and it unwound in a reluctant twirl.

'That's one,' she said.

'You're good at this,' said the boy. 'I usually have a box that I stand on for high branches, but it got blown away.'

She didn't ask him why he hung the shoes on the tree. Joe would have approved. He always said, "focus on the task, not the reason." It was one of the few things she had disagreed with him about and did most mornings when she woke up and felt the daily gnawing of grief.

'Which are your new shoes?'

'They're gone,' said the boy. 'I put them up, and they'd disappeared by the next day. It didn't matter though.'

He smiled, and Sheila-Ann thought that he looked younger, as if his face had been rubbed clean of anxiety.

'Dad told me I should see it as a sign. I didn't need those brand-new shoes for good luck. Old and scruffy would do the trick'.

'He's right,' Sheila-Ann said. 'Something worn out has been on a journey. Made discoveries. It's never an ending.'

She smiled at the difference between what she'd said and how she'd lived during the last year. Small and protective, like a snail in her shell. Joe would have said that at last she was learning.

The boy swung his arms round and round, like he was getting ready to fly before turning to her and bowing.

'Rory,' he said.

She thought the name suited his orange jacket and the curls of auburn hair that weren't hidden by his beanie. She bowed back and said, 'Sheila-Ann.'

He nodded and there was another glimpse of his smile.

'My dad said, "find shoes that played football games every Saturday, ran by the river or had gone on holidays." So that's what I did.'

He walked round the other side of the tree and pointed to a pair of black trainers, with the soles hanging off like leathery tongues.

'These belong to Archie who helps me at school when I can't manage lessons. They've trekked across the desert and been covered in African sand, which is millions of years old and was trampled on by dinosaurs. We both liked that.'

Sheila-Ann stretched up and touched the heel of one of the trainers and spun it slowly.

'Do you think there's still a trickle of sand in them?' she said.

'I checked,' said Rory. 'Only the tiniest speck.'

She reached towards a pink and blue shoe that hung by itself on a lower branch and untwisted it, so it hung straight and swayed in the quietening breeze. 'And this one?'

'That's from my pal, Star. She said I could have one because she wanted to hang the other one in her garden. It's special because she ran a race when nobody thought she could. She got a medal and was in the papers.'

'Then one is enough,' said Sheila-Ann.

'Exactly what I thought. She cleaned it specially so it could hang here.'

They'd circled the tree three times now. There was a rhythm to their walking, Rory walking next to the trunk, and Sheila-Ann keeping pace on the outside.

She stopped. 'There are ten pairs of shoes plus Star's one. Do you know all the stories?'

Rory picked up his stick and prodded the heel of a trainer that had the face of a cat painted on the front.

'Yup. Sometimes I tell the stories to myself, so I remember. This one belonged to my neighbour, Shireen, who said that she'd grown out of cat shoes, and was going to get lace up boots that made her look like a teenager with attitude. I thought I'd like to do that one day too.' He stopped. 'Maybe not yet.'

He pointed to a pair of shoes that were smaller than the rest. Sparkly and red with tiny heels.

'One day when I got here there was a woman hanging shoes. She said they were her daughter's and she needed something good to happen because her little girl was poorly and in hospital. She thought this was a special tree too.'

'Like a clootie tree,' said Sheila-Ann. 'Where people hang a piece of cloth for good luck. Healing.'

The moment she said "healing", she felt the word had come out wrong, but Rory grinned.

'That's it. Except they're shoes. Which is better because anyone can hang shoes here.' He looked at Sheila-Ann. 'Dad said I shouldn't get the wrong idea. I didn't need luck. I just needed…' Rory patted the trunk of the tree. 'Distraction.'

She looked at Rory and felt something shift in her stomach. Like a rock had been pushed out of the way, letting a flood of blood move around her body.

'I'll see if I can get higher,' she said.

She took off her jacket and reached up to the thickest branch. She could feel the roughness of the bark sharp against her fingertips, and she moved them until there was a patch of lichen. Her feet swung off the ground for a moment, and the branch creaked. She tried to grasp one of the red shoes with her fingers, but it bounced away, and she let her feet drop back on the ground.

'Nearly,' she said.

Rory clapped his hands. Bloom had stretched out next to him and closed his eyes. Sheila-Ann sucked at a scratch where her thumb had caught on a thorn.

'Does that hurt?' he said.

She shook her head. 'It's nothing.'

She sat down and leaned against the trunk of the hawthorn. It wasn't comfortable. More like the back of a hard chair, that didn't yield but held you up. Her heart was beating as fast as it wanted. It was a flashing reminder of the exhilaration she'd got from climbing a hill or paddling to the far end of a loch. She and Rory sat in silence while the breeze pushed the shoes around. Every so often there was a thud as the shoes collided.

The sun began to disappear behind the trees, and Sheila-Ann felt a stiffness in her arms as if they'd been tugged as far as they would go and then given back to her. She pushed herself up on her feet and watched Rory stroke Bloom.

'I've got a pair of old boots that need somewhere to go,' she said. 'Can I hang them on the tree?'

Rory nodded. 'I'll be here tomorrow. Will there be a story?'

'Yes,' Sheila-Ann said, and wondered which one she would tell. ᴋʀ

Nocturne

Barry Smith

As I watch you sleeping,
see your breasts rise and fall,
I hear the tree moaning,
grasping in the wind
and clasping in the sky
as your hand clutches the sheet.

You, you are silent restful,
far from the tree that groans,
you cannot hear it raking the sky
and I, telescope of all
sounds and sense impressions,
am seared by them all.

Your flesh is hot and burning,
your brow white, white hot –
you stir in your sleep –
but the wind, it is there
still curling
through the tree and the sky.

The wind, it will cool you,
infiltrate your sleep
and you will carry
the imprint of the night
tomorrow, when you wake.

Echoes

Bells that toil through the snow
confirm the absence of the sun,
white powder and grey dust
trace the way we have gone;
clouds that stretch across the sky today
form the backcloth of the skyscape,
russet and orange, violet and green,
shapeshift across your hazy sight.

Roar of the city and gusts of the downs
are smothered in gathering stillness
and the faces, pallid or bronzed,
crumble to nothing in your dreams;
do you tire of these gaudy illuminations,
and do you tire of yourself, child of neon,
child of clay, child of the evening,
does your light refract in stuttering echoes
and return in sharp fragments
as you watch the faces in the room?

She has stood in a hall of mirrors,
arms full of flowers,
posing attitudes gracefully
and failed to choose her image,
stepped from frame to frame
and passed distantly into the evening,
hear the echo, the echo,
self and self echoing through the hollow room. ᴋᴿ

Gail Webb

Creation

At first I want you everywhere,
a place at the formica table,
or next to me, watching TV.
Space to soak in the bath,
your head at the tap end.
Our toes touch in the suds.
You are silent, never express
how you feel. I am the leader.

I have to explain you to others:
She is there, right there.
You smile as if enjoying
the lack of attention.
It irritates me, the way others
overlook your presence.
Secret smiles slide into each other—
a place is set for you at tea.

Gradually, they disappear you.
Your none- entity is outed daily,
easy to do, as you have no voice,
no body, no clothes.
I am asked—once or twice—
about your likes and dislikes.
The phrase 'special friend'
is thrown about like an old doll.

She has gone I announce,
pleased with the way I hide
my distress. *She has found a new home*
where they want her, much better than here.
Mam looks confused, slightly put out.
The dinner plate with your name is put away.
I sometimes take it out, trace the letters.
Here I am, without you. **KR**

Snowdrops

Stop.

First up, painted, could be (on paper)
upstroke to a tail.

Balled white. Faithful.

Woodside, all-bright, arm-linked, in brambles.

Church folk, hatted: belief holds them up.

Look.

Fold-outs sprouting.

Impacts, fistfuls, shreds come together.

God-spots, fallen.

Beginnings, outfalls, crumbs on water.

Pond-skin kick-backs, drips along the path.

Listen.

Bells and shakers and Oms in the head.

Air-pressed repeats on joined-together headphones.

Wind chimes, flowering.

Oh what a splash.

ESOL

The teacher says verbs. We travel.

On the wall's a set of rules
and a blown-up atlas,

it's a forced march, flags on a map,
a series of arrivals.

Words are sails,
skin-thin and billowing
they sing and stretch

and run before the wind;

odd-voiced, quirky,
they flap and tear free.

Taped-up, labelled, bordered,
the world is on the walls.

Learning is an action:
I see. I try. I speak.

In a corner there is laugher.
Up and down voices circle print.

The walls have mouths,
delicate, determined
they battle through checkpoints and barriers.

Ideas touch down like long-delayed flights.

Solar Panel

This page left open,
being read by the sun,
begins a new chapter.

Line-ruled and squared
it's an economics textbook.

Inside this box
there are brightly-lit photos
of faces in a circle
holding flowers and candles
in a festival of light.

On dull days it reminds us
of heatstroke, ice loss and
scorched-earth habitats
and the land under siege
from overspill and drought

of life under the hammer
sliced and diced by on-screen dealers
and driven to the brink by
split-second, money-grabbing traders.

And now in the open, in the clear,
a mirror held up.

Seen from above
it's a raft out to sea
holding a small cargo
of earth and seedlings

or a placard on a march
arm in arm, moving in silence
to pace out the kingdom

or a photo held up
of Earth through time
from single cell to spiral and growth
then bright and alive and smiley,
spread by chance,
and linked by angels to the sun. ᴋʀ

Sue Lewis

Six Months Below

Dark days almost over

he must camouflage
his desperate longing for her

cover it with leaves

for winter cannot hold her
while the world above her waits

though sky is blank, snow-scented
sleeping hedges silver-brown

her wheat will rise to green and gold
& sooner than they think

he has to let her go now

she has everything she needs
& he can't fasten her with words
(or even pomegranate seeds)
no matter how he tries

calm, so calm this gentle morning
see the snowdrops?
both of them might start again ᴋʀ

The Afterlife

assume existence isn't absurd

MARK GODFREY

His relationship with the afterlife had always been a complicated one. Not that he struggled to believe, he simply wasn't sure of the best means to get there. What gnawed away at him wasn't whether or not to check out early, by means of pills or a noose or stepping off a railway platform in front of the 12.55 to Glasgow—he was quite relaxed at having to wait patiently for the present life to come to a natural end—no, the real source of his anxiety, a state of mind that was becoming more acute as the years advanced, was who to choose for company on the journey.

He'd tried religion, in fact he'd tried several, and each had come up short. Where he'd hoped for affirmation and joy and a sense of being surrounded by the love and understanding of fellow souls on a joyous but solemn transport from one life to another, he found rules and rituals and hyperbolic texts and a tendency to be too much in awe of only one side of the story. The other sticking point was God: it wasn't an outright lack of faith; he just didn't think there could be so many of Him.

By early mid-life, his religious phase behind him, he found himself in thrall to people who advised him to live in the moment—a state of mind he disliked and preferred not to acknowledge—and wondered if the way to eternity was destined to be a lonely one. He cast around social media, imagining there would be many people, like him, waiting for this life to expire and the next to materialise—or etherealise, as he would joke to himself. But apparently not: on offer was a depressingly moribund collection of humanity that, despite taking in the full spectrum from pragmatists to fantasists, contained not a single non-denominational devotee of the unearthly paradise, or so it seemed.

What he didn't expect was what he found on his doorstep one day. Quite literally. Visitors were rare, and at the sound of the doorbell one evening he rose hesitantly and suspiciously to answer. Peering through the crack of the barely opened door, he saw a young woman with a document bag and an I.D. card hanging round her neck. He cursed himself for not having the gumption to ignore the call. Now he was trapped; she would want to sign him up for a regular donation and not take no for an answer. Getting rid of her would be a painful, prolonged process.

But she didn't look dangerous, and he found himself opening the door, even though he would have liked to slam it shut.

'Yes,' he said.

'I won't bite,' she said. He hated it when people said this.

'Pity,' he said. It was a reflex; out of his mouth before he'd even thought it, and where it had come from he had no idea.

She paused and stared at him. For a moment he sensed he'd thrown her off her stride, and he felt the initiative pass to him.

'Would you like to come in?' he said.

Her smiling face reconstructed itself apprehensively.

'I won't bite,' he said, pleased with the reversal and surfing a blissful and unfamiliar wave of confidence.

He smiled, she almost laughed, and it was enough to get her inside.

Two months later, lying in bed with her head nestled into his shoulder, he wondered if it was a suitable moment to initiate a discussion about the afterlife. He'd hedged around it enough, dotting his conversation with phrases such as, 'maybe in the next life,' 'next time I hope to come back as a cat,' and, following a latex and role-play sex marathon, 'I think I've died and gone to heaven,' but there had been no take up on her part.

He asked if she believed in life after death. She asked, what on earth had prompted him to ask that. He said it was something he thought about most of the time.

'In that case why have you never mentioned it before?'

As he lay on his back, watching a fly cross the ceiling, he feared that a lot may hinge on what he said next.

'It's very personal,' he said.

'Lots of people believe in life after death,' she said, 'it's nothing to be ashamed of.'

She teased him that he'd felt 'silly' in raising it. He confessed to being more obsessed with the idea than most people.

'But how do you know?' she said, and he admitted that he didn't. 'Especially if other people are as reluctant to broach the subject as you are.'

He told her he understood her logic, but he reckoned that on a scale of one to ten he was ten plus whereas most people were about a five.

'So, do you?' he said.

'Do I what?' she said.

'Believe in an afterlife,' he said, before adding, 'keep up.' He gave her a squeeze to emphasise the humorous tone he very much hoped he'd conveyed.

She asked if the afterlife and life after death were the same thing.

It was a wonderful moment to hear her discriminate between the two. He'd switched his reference from one to the other because he assumed most people would see them as synonymous. And when he'd said "life after death" he was merely opening up a conversation that could be defined more precisely if, by happy chance, she entered into it in the spirit he'd hoped.

'No!' he blurted out, with such a dramatic flourish that he immediately apologised.

She asked why he used the terms interchangeably if he was so sure they weren't the same thing.

'Is it because you thought I was stupid?' she said.

'Of course not,' he said. He begged her to believe him when he said he felt a joy unconfined at her wish to take him up on the semantics of the matter.

'So, what is the difference?' she said.

'Life after death implies a future as a living entity,' he said, 'such as coming back as a toad or something, whereas the afterlife is the transcendence into a higher state of being.'

'That's what I thought,' she said.

'So?' he said.

'So what?' she said.

'So, do you believe in the afterlife, or in life after death?'

'Tell me why it's so important to you,' she said.

After a few weeks she moved in, bringing with her a modest collection of belongings—clothes, jewellery, pictures, some kitchen stuff, no furniture—and new ideas about how to organise the home.

'It's important to prepare for the afterlife,' she said, 'by making our material home the incarnation of our spirit home.'

And so she set to work, rearranging the furniture, creating a meditation space, painting the walls, bringing in flowers and fruit bowls and candles and scents, and all the while talking of the afterlife as though it were a loving and faithful friend.

'Honey, what do you think the afterlife looks like?' she said, one day.

He told her he thought it might be more a case of what it feels like.

'Would it feel like heroin,' she said, 'but without the downside; an endless natural high?'

'I've never done heroin,' he said, and then looked at her, worried for something that may have happened in her past, 'have you?'

She asked him why he wanted to know, and he said he didn't really. But he picked up her arm to examine it. She tutted but yielded to his inspection. All he found was perfect, milky-white skin, the soft smoothness of which he followed to her shoulder and her neck and into her eyes.

'Maybe it's like an endless sexual high,' he said.

'A never-ending orgasm?' she said.

'It's why sex and death are so entwined in life,' he said, 'although I imagine the afterlife to be less energetic.'

She teased him that he imagined cotton-ball clouds and lush valleys with fruit trees and people playing the lute with haloes round their heads. He lied and said he imagined a giant theme park with candy stalls where people could eat as much as they wanted and never fear getting fat.

'Because they're already dead,' he said.

Secretly, he wondered if she believed in the afterlife at all. Everything she said seemed a provocation, as though testing him, screening him, and, though he dared not admit it in so many words, quietly, insidiously mocking him.

Earlier in the relationship she would say things that seemed charming, that helped create a sanctity in which they set themselves apart from the world and celebrated the uniqueness of their union. But now these little statements maybe carried a false air. During a fine meal she would say, 'I can almost taste the afterlife', or while picnicking in the countryside, lying on her back, staring into the blue sky,

'I can almost see the afterlife'. According to her, the afterlife was everywhere, and he didn't quite believe her anymore.

'Is it wrong I should share your obsession?' she said.

He'd blundered in, not really preparing himself for a confrontation he feared he was ill-equipped to carry off, but at least he'd put the issue out there.

'But do you?' he said, steeling himself to stand his ground though torturing himself in the process.

It didn't work. He was reduced to admitting it was based on a 'feeling', that he 'sensed' something not right, that his 'instinct' had made him doubt.

'What if you're wrong?' she said, 'your feeling, sense and instinct all lying; and aren't these intuitions the basis of your belief in the afterlife?' He gulped for an answer, but she continued, 'what if it's me who truly believes in the afterlife?'

He wanted to believe: in her and in the afterlife.

'I'm sorry,' he said, 'it's so important to me; I get anxious about it sometimes.'

That night, the wound in his faith healed, they lay in bed after sex.

'I think I glimpsed the afterlife,' she said.

'It certainly was good,' he said.

'No,' she said, 'I mean I really saw the afterlife, just for a second, right in the middle, before you got your arm tangled up in the pillowcase.'

He propped himself up and looked at her. The wound threatened to open again, but her face had an aura: she glowed, and she was happier than he'd ever seen her.

'What was it like?' he said.

'It was a feeling, just as you said. A feeling you could almost see, if that makes sense. It was like nothing else.'

For days he railed against the injustice. Why her? A newbie; someone whose faith he'd had reason to doubt. Why not him, the disciple of so many years, the true believer, the ten plus on the scale, the person whose every fibre has quivered in anticipation of that glimpse?

She made him tea and dispensed sympathy, all the while telling him how undeserving she was and that she would give it up for him in a flash if she could.

'It's not fair,' he said.

'Life isn't,' she said, 'I got lucky.'

One day, while they were feeding ducks in the park, she told him she had a plan. She would help him glimpse the afterlife, but he would have to trust her unhesitatingly and absolutely or it wouldn't work.

He was more than a little intrigued, and though sceptical—a fact he kept to himself in order not to be found in breach of the absolute trust rule—and in spite her refusal to give further detail, he agreed to her 'experiment'.

And so, one night he arrived home to find her wearing a bright white leotard and the meditation space strewn with mats and cushions. There was something sweetly acrid in the air and she wore a gold chain and jewelled headdress that wrapped around and fitted to her head like a skullcap. She stood in the doorway, smiling coquettishly, and he wondered if he dare ask if this was the moment he'd been waiting for.

'Welcome to the afterlife,' she said, pre-empting him, as though impatient to get things moving.

She made him lie among the cushions, his questions ignored or shushed.

'Absolute trust,' she said, whispering into his ear and flicking it with her tongue as an afterthought.

She had oil, she had perfume, and she had her hands. She peeled off his clothing, she scented the cushions, and she oiled his body in stages as the parts of him became naked. She was slow and methodical, breathing heavily, exhaling onto his neck and his chest, teasing his oil softened skin with her lips.

He wanted to ask how this could lead to the afterlife—wasn't this simply the present life, although a heavenly version of it?—but he daren't interrupt her flow; she had a plan, he told himself, so he would play his part and cede to her.

She wriggled from her leotard and straddled him. She'd done her work, and he was desperate to enter her, but she teased him further, prolonging the moment until he was spinning with desire.

Then she tied it around his neck: her lanyard, the one her ID had hung from the day they first met. He was in her now and as she rode him, she tightened it, wrapping it around her forefinger and turning on his neck like a tourniquet.

As his breathing constricted, the pleasure overrode the pain, and he heard her shouting for him to say when he'd seen the afterlife. She rode him faster and turned tighter, and he felt something drain in his head. In the spasmodic rush that followed, as the warm wash of ecstasy gathered and exploded, convulsing him, and as his consciousness gave out to the blackening void, he glimpsed the afterlife. He tried to call out, but his voice had left his body and, dimly, in a final receding thought before he was gone, he knew that in choosing her he'd chosen well. ᴋʀ

Scattering the ashes

Asking the wind
you know how sometimes
you catch a leaf
on its final fall
in some invisible fire blanket
transformed to trampoline
giving one last gift
of being bird?

And you know sometimes
if we go too fast
as we enter the woods
you can suddenly still
make the birds disappear
until we are still too
or until we are gone?

Well…

Phil Madden

The three last breaths becoming

The one that leaves.
The last fledgling.
May make the sea.
May be blown on the rocks.

The one that stays.
Gets as far as the lips.
Looks out.
Sighs back.

The one that looks in.
Sees the state of things.

Heart search

It is cold. No one else here.
Heart searching for patterns.
Life, of course, and the river running its.
And a heron. Reminding me how to wait.
The pattern comes. I pick pennant sandstones.
The blue stilling.

Your heart searched the air.
Could find no red.
You are cold now. 'At rest', we say.
Blood stilled to blue. No one else there.

It is cloudy.
Blue above it.

Shrugs. Turns back. ꓘꓤ

Angela Arnold

Landmarks

Straight up the plump mound, across the full
warmth of it. On, down to a point
where ribs congregate—essential scaffolding.

Follow another cutting across,
lower, more livid, never
really stilled.

Odd roads, dips, wells, harmless
protuberances—a confused map.
One that'll keep (pain on pain) growing;

that can't guarantee
parts of it won't be snatched
away, crossed out

any time soon: loss of a whole precious
catalogue of mishaps, knocks,
cruel scrapes… heroic encounters,

some of them. All that writing:
the full, whole, intimate account,
in every detail, meticulous,

practically filed. Flesh diaries.
What better evidence of time spent
with, among, on earth **KR**

Patricia Helen Wooldridge

Epiphany

The woods
if not heading to the woods
then walking alongside the fringeline
ground ivy spilling into light pools
gaps in the canopy
the woods give us bones   what we strip down to
the bones that knit into webs of sky
come here   winter light   brief day

and what happens in the dark
when you are not there
to enter woodland at night   the tawny owl
reading the paths held in the air…
you are indoors listening to the call
as she travels tree to tree   let us
walk outside   keep to the edge
come here   winter dark   long night

Stepping away from self

daisy
thistledown
uncut grass

undercover
in the side street
of her mind

the open curtain time
between day and evening
leaves washed to a tideline

if there were thoughts
they left on a pink dusk
such as this

weeds rooted in the gutter
the aftertaste of smoke
webs grazed in dew

The Dark Horse

There is a grace that comes
when watching a horse grazing…
the stillness of a stand in October's
green with head down feeding

while the tail keeps to some largo
tempo to brush its flank…
I am mesmerised every time
and mostly the horses are

in their own world—except today
one dark horse stands apart
listening to us passing down
the track we call 'spindle lane'

for here there are fine spindle trees.
We rest on the gate scanning the view
turn to see the dark horse trotting up
the rise towards us—

she stands at the gate wanting
contact—we let her smell our hands
for any horse needs time to judge
our scent, our voice, our touch.

Dark horse lets me stroke her
listens as I talk quiet words
full of admiration for this tall
seemingly gentle large horse.

I leave and feel the emotion
of some lost parting. ꓦꓤ

memory goes on

Adam Craig

nexttime

don't say, don't look, don't say, don't say
that voice, that look, reminds, remembers, feel it, feel it remembering
that way, can't, don't, don't do that, don't do, can't breathe can't forget,
twisting, don't, that way that voice that face like that hand always that
hand always, always that, reminding, shaking, sweat sweating can't stop
shaking, *don't do that*, that standing, standing like like   that, don't say
don't use, breathe, don't use that tone say, don't those words, that face,
breathe, don't moving breath voice, don't standing closer closering like,
breathe can't breathe, remembering, it's here, now here, see it, can't
breathe can't no no, nodon't, feel comingcloser twisting can't breathe
shaking, that stand, don't thatway, always that way remembering
reminding becoming, againing that always, thatway shaking, breathe
can'tbreathe don't, don't, saidtold already said goaway, can't help, look
don'tlook, don't touch that way remembering, handloom and facetwist
and shoulders shaking, going to puke can'tbreathe can'tstand, *no*, said
didn'ti said alreadysaidbefore toldbefore, not you not you notyounot
younotyou, can't breathe, rememberfeel remembersee all hereandnow,
shapeinthewindow, openwindow like that, shut the window, no, no, no
don'tshut because, stand away, remember, don't be in the window, no, no
forget, can'tforget, inhead and ingut, just away and breathe, breathe,
breathe, face wet can't breathe, that sigh that look   did did *did*
lookandsigh, can't breathe, can't look that look standing here

alwayshere, it's always here, inskull, inme muscle and tremble and reminding and
shaking and sweating and swaying and and not, not forget can'tforget, can'tstant
can'tgo, don't do that, don't, don't be that, don'tdo, don't, not, never, don't, leave
the window, go away, remember the window and the shape making black and
shape closerandcloser, shape you, isn't it you, said already, remember, remember
shape, stand back don'tcan'thelp can't help remembering shape shape here here
shape here now don't lie don't say don't say words and lies and is here shapehere
right here *here* don't make me don't make me can't help can't can't can't can't
don't don't makeme don't don't   DON'T

                                                                head
head feel   feels   wrong and door slamming, wrong fit   footsteps out,
outside in, in the corridor, badfitting mouth, wrongfitting teeth in the corridor,
steps, footsteps in the corridor, doorshut slammed in silence, almost silent head,
sting stinging, neck, shoulders, twisted and hand, hands, trembling, in the
breeze   window open, swung back, wideswung, swinging to hit, hit, hit the
wall, left open, dent, a siren going, gone by and horns, a dent in the wall, and
horns and the traffic hitting against, against the breeze against the dent, in the
wall, against the siren gone going by, against the ringing and the acheandthrob,
painthrob, blood and heart and tremor, muscle and lungs turn, turned, turning
into throb   jawclick, jaw clicking, siren passing   hands   shaking: want
to die: underbreath, words halfheard, halftrue, jawclicking over each piece of
each wordhissed underbreath: want you to die   can't stand   not this not
anymore   can't stand, can't move, not yet and the room, eyestung and don'tcry,
room throbs, in, time to siren, wrongfeel of mouth and the, swell, swell of
cheekthrob   rocking   knees weak, legs fixed to chair chair fixed to floor
floorfixed and throbbing   better   if   don't come   back   come back
           handleturned, door opening, swung, swinging slam on the breeze, on
the wall, room startling, no footsteps, no liftnoise, no keysound scraped in the
lock, onlygasp, only doorslam, hand overmouthed, against the wall
           siren   gone   can't just   no   listen: you
know it   don't come any closer   listen: know, you know, know
how   don't, don't come closer just, just stay   we must talk,
sorry take, take my hand   flinch, breath short, sob, don't, don't, don't
hover   fixed inside the doorway, door closing and watching, rubbing
feeling back intohand   don't, please, explained before, said, it's not not,
don't say, don't cry, don't please, just talk   breathshort   trembling
           don't hover, don't watch so, haven't you, haven't, haven't you   turning
away, from door, room skewing with turning, window widing, arm on the hand

of the chair, hand, hand on the arm of the chair, white hand with knuckles, ashhand with red, trembling window, hand trembling with the room and the window, open the window open and letting in traffic noise, in bruises, breezes, not, not bruises, breezes   *don't look*   just don't, haven't you seen, just stay, back, just *leave me*   dog bark, barking next door, nextdoor's dog starting to bark, the wall barking   fuck fucking dog, slamming a palm of the hand against the wall between this and the dog, fucking dog all it does, *shut up yapping*, all that dog does is bark and yip, fucking thing, can't you shut *up*?

    SHUT UP   handslammed the wall sounds thin, hollowthin jaw click with next breath, don't take it out on   baby crying other nextdoor, dog, dog barking, crying, footsteps in the corridor outside   lifts the hand flinchturn away, onewall crying, onewall barking, hornsound, traffichorning and revving, otherhand pounding onewall, otherwall, shutupping and growing red and breathless, upset upsetting in panic   *please*, don't just please   ringingears pound pound head and lip, room cold, trembling, open window open breeze open mouth   just   talk if you talk but don't those those things the loud the voice loud saying and pounding, if you talk just talk what you   dog barking   a sigh and talking, through the walls the open window the closed door, noone taking a step, standing, just, just leaning, the chair with white hands that tremble

                      look, look listen, it's a fault, noone's fault it's, can't, can't say sorry again, againandagains but sorry, not your fault, not myfault either is it, no no no it's   baby barking crying traffic engines gears and grinding between the ears and a door open shut shut between the ears, room, this room, little room, a chair, sniffing, the room sniffing, might rain later   blame is is what, saying it's not, not only, not me not just me, understand, you, you must because it's not justme it's what happened isn't it see you need to understand because you you you do you you babydoghornsoutsideintheroadoutsidehornsoutside   SHUT   UP   just shut, shut   look, just, we should, should we could we   please, don't we try, just help, just can't, see, you have, to have, to understand it was is it just it will yes, see   bloodinmouth, bloodspit, tissue red, fingerknuckle red

      please   room feels sicksour, room feels too dizzy to stand, too dizzy to sit, and blood from mouth as shape, as a shape comes away from the door no harm, not harm, didn't mean, mean didn't mean any, any, just understand nodding, shrugging, hating, the room hates and nods and feels tears and a stomachtight sour and has the taste of copper in it, and a smell of iron any harm   no, none

the room
can't move, only the breeze and the breeze says it can't go on the breeze says: i
can't go on and you says the breeze and the window open you says the room you
need help fucking help don't care don't can't can't   yes you, you've,
you've a, it's natural say, to be, but   don't start not just   dogs and
babies and the traffic always going going always   please can't we, can't
we pretend, no, not pretend, just   the room tastes iron and copper and
sour and feels numb and the room feels dizzy and as it stands the window is
always open but all the room lets in is the same the same the room is always
letting in aches in each joint and a chair with white hands and the room, the
room sighs, and the room, the room whispers: get past this   yes past,
yes, not fault, tea, yes hot, hot tea, how about   tea makes everything   better,
yes, so   room does, does not, move, room looks, does not look, looks
into a corner of itself aware, not aware, of a shape by the door, shape not part of
the room and coming closer, chairpressed, pressing chair pressing, a hand,
pressing a hand to its arm and, and trying to stand on its, feet   it, it's
just you, you know, just a memory a thing a thing in the past it's, not youorme,
not us is it us it's the past, can't you, we, us get on, over, get over past the past
babystopped   dogstopped   nothing   else   tea then

          shrug, roomshrugs, and bruises in the
light, the light from the window, standing and shaky next to the window
sorry   sighs underbreath the room says: don't say sorry sorry whatgood
is   did you say, with the kettle, the kettle going, can't hear, did you say
     no   windowopen, open and pressing into the room's thighs, the
room's muscles trembling stomach, and stomach, sour and sick, bilerising, can't
stand straight, can't sit can't stand can't stand this can't   this room is so empty

     drink your tea
         the room is silent but for
steam and scaldinghot against a shaking hand, teasurface slopsloshing
careful you'll scald   don't want tea, drink tea, slurp and   laugh, room
a short laugh: no biscuits?   what, no, there isn'tany   the room
watches steam rise and the shape get lower, becoming sitting on the edge of the
lip of that other chair in another part of this room   you   angry,
the room is angry in this between one breath and next breath and knuckles turn
white on squeezing the scalding hot mug   you   fucking pig you could have
fucking said before before before went to the fucking fuck shops before, before

this   you don't ever fucking think   splash and spatter tea across the
room's floor, room's foot   and the shape, the shape sighs and stands and
tells the room hush it's only biscuits it's not anything to worry, no worrying
about and the stain and the floor   and the room is going is going, to, is
going to throw, the scalding, the teamug scalding at   at   that's your
favourite mug   don't love you, don't everneverdid, don't   don't it, it's
notlike   just, just putdown the mug, please   don'tlove you
      i know   don't love   i know, don't move, get a cloth, might
rain, later, rain might be have had, hasn't had, rain, hasn't for for, some, for
somewhile   don't love you   drink up, i know, what's left
bark, dogging through the walls, and babymoan, sirenagain, only fading, horn,
and traffic, and window, open, swollen, and tender, big against the room's tongue,
breath short, not soshort   drink up and later, later makefresh, promise
      nexttime   and biscuits, pop, pop out, pop out to the shops, now
and   ok   years can pass this way, jawclick clicking, left, right,
leftright   roadsilent   dog silent, babysilence almost toppling over, to stoop
missed a bit   coming to rest on the room's floor, two knees on the floor and a
hand on the floor and a tissue in another hand, to mop, spillage cold
no need, don't, it'll be mop, latermopped, you shouldn't, shouldn't leave, don't
leave, just leave that for later, later mopping   please   bruise isn't so
bad, thinks the room   ok   leave, yes, all, it'll sort, mop and tea and
biscuits, going to go now, if   if   yes, okay, says the room watching tea
grow dry in a patch on the floor of the room watching the tea and saying yes
and saying after a moment: and teabags, must remember bags, remember,
youknow, at the shop the corner shop, and cleanerspray and don't forgot biscuits
and paracetemol   yes   back inamoment   take a
coat   might later, rain, to the shop, and get paracetamol and ovenchips for
dinner if you want ovenchips, want dinner   you cook? me?
doesn't matter   later   yesalright, later   together   go now,
might later, rain
                              door closing and standing by the window,
openwindow standing and watching down, down at the hand on the
windowframe at the street   lip still aches, stillaching, siren and traffic and
carhorns   a shape   watching, as it goes to the corner, shop, cornershop,
memories, seen this before, all before, a twitching nerve in the room and
headache and sourtaste in mouth, walls brittle and the floor, the floor is stained
and unsteady, every muscle in every chair aches and the light, the light in the
ceiling, that aches and that, that needs, it needs to pee, or puke, cold spit,

coldsour, each one, each memory, a memory before, before nexttime   first rain,
spot, spots against, glass, against the face, windowpane face, windows have no
face, the traffic goes, better sometimes, no dogbark no babycry nosiren,
nowandthen therain, not allthewhile, this, not allthewhile, just when, when the
wordsmemoriesfeelings, when the room, this room could be worse   the wind
touches the glass windowsways and reflects and sways so the room sees itself in
the window, not allthewhile, just when   could be worse, could be better,
bebetter tomorrow   itwill   it couldbe   windowsay   this is the
room   this is what the room   babyquite dogquite trafficneverquiet

                                                                    shape
on the pavement, again   but next nexttime, gethelp or getbetter
hand at eyelevel, room's hand not shaking somuch, room's knees weak but that
liftsounds, sound of the lift lifting   spot on the floor stilldamp, won't probably
stain, no reminder

                                              door turns its handle and the room
lets in the door which says brought biscuits and ovenchips and beansandpeas
and freshloaf nicesliced freshloaf and don't, don't, don't do that, don't scrub,
scrub the floor so there's, there's no, no need   just justrying
no, let me, let me dothat and you dodinner, yes, you dodinner and i bought wine,
look wine, not expensive, so better, yes, better nexttime, drink to that nexttime,
promise, so let, me, letme, promise me you'll letme, else, i'll else, else i'll   you
know   don't say that   wrist bare, sleeve wet pulled away,
taking the damp cloth, damp sleeve, damp skin, skin scarred at the wrists   i'll
i can't stop help can't it's   sorry, but   don't   clean and you
cook and then open wine and   and   pull the window, yes, window pull to
and nexttime, won't it, nexttime, we'll   we'll see, yes

rain against the glass, against the floor, silent, almost silence, traffic lights on
green, amberlight on the cooker, amber notred   we could watch, you
know, we, we could, could watch, wiping at the floor and wristhidden bycoat by
mopping, we you know you know you like that you know that you know you like
that yes so while, while so, time passes and we watch and drink wine and time
passes   I'll   the oven is hot and the food will cook and the light in
the bathroom flickers and in the bathroom cabinet there are painkillers and
antiseptic and razorblades and plasters and when the mirror closes there is a face
and it is the room's face and there are eyes and it is the room looking, looking
intoeyes, and there is saying: yes, yes let's watch, let's sit and watch and then
everything will, will everything be, and the eyes of the room look into the eyes of

the room and the room's eyes admit they are eyes not room notroom and eyes
and face everything nexttime, everything will could, and the eyes are wet and the
white hands turn the tap and the splash of water is not tears or spit or sourtaste
in this mouth and bruising, and looking, intomirror intoeyes, there is there, a
room around doorclosed, there there is, this, only, onlythis, and there there is

only **KR**

Contributor biographies

ANGELA ARNOLD has been creative all her life, as writer, poet, painter, smallholder and creative gardener. She now lives in Wales, with a lot of trees for neighbours, and grows bee-friendly flowers and small amounts of food that give her huge delight. She is a member of the local XR group and is learning Welsh, a language that has you relating to the world around you differently.

YVONNE BAKER lives on the borders of Hampshire and Sussex and her poems often include its landscape. She writes mostly around themes of identity, the inner life and home. She's an avid reader, which provides an inspiration for writing. Yvonne has been published in print and on-line magazines. Her work has been included in *Second Light, Paper Swans, Emma Press and Poetry Space* anthologies.

ADAM CRAIG writes about place, a lot: interior spaces, external locations, real, imagined… His novels and short fiction often bring place in as character, or enter into dialogue with places, sometimes combatively, sometimes cooperatively. He suspects that no place is ever a fixed thing but always the consequence of emotion, history and viewpoint. Maybe people are the same. This what he writes about.

SUSAN ELSLEY says: I write stories about people and places. My short and long fiction reflects a deep commitment to natural and wilder environments, and is often set in places which can promote healing but also reveal the sharpness of the world. I live by the sea in Scotland and go north and west whenever I can. *susanelsley.com*

MICK EVANS writes: I grew up in Hertfordshire, London overspill. My paternal ancestry is Welsh, maternal English. For half my life home has been Wales' fertile Towy Valley. Garn Goch's Bronze Age settlement squats on the skyline. Over the Black Mountain, end of the Brecon Beacons, begins the industrial past. My writing life is a struggle to reconcile contrasting histories, welling up, spilling over these hills.

JAN FORTUNE lives in a surviving area of ancient forest in Finistère, where she writes novels and poetry, edits books and mentors writers. She is currently training as a herbalist practitioner and her work in progress is inspired by the local forest and her conversations with plants.

MARK GODFREY is the author of the novel, *The River Reflects* (Cinnamon Press). He lives in Greater Manchester, with his wife, an eminent art curator. They have two grown up children, three granddaughters and a grandson.

KATE GOUGH is a Californian writer and artist currently living in North Wales. Her practice is both flighty and deep. She is wildly in love with the world, and stokes that love with words. Kate has written and exhibited for newspapers, litmags, galleries, spoken word events, and touring exhibitions around the UK and the USA. Her work can be found in *Flash Fiction Magazine, Wild Roof Journal*, and *Peregrine Journal*.

ISABELLE LLASERA was born of French parents in London. She has worked in Scotland, China, England, Spain and France, teaching, training teachers and organising cultural events. She published her short story collection, *Smog*, with Cinnamon Press in 2020.

SUE LEWIS is from South London. Her poetry explores the texture of life; her close observation finds the beauty even within her urban environment. She practises qigong and walks every day. She won the Cinnamon pamphlet prize in 2019 with *Texture* and in 2021 with *Journey* and was shortlisted for the Bridport poetry prize in 2022.

PHIL MADDEN writes: Being centred and changing and adapting. I try each day to breathe the sky and for me to find 'Path as somewhere along the way here I am'. Whatever the weather, whatever the mood, wherever the eye falls let it notice.

KATE NOAKES says: I write from both the city and the country, having a geographer's and an artist's eye. I live in London, but spend time in Wales, where my family has it roots, and the West country where I was brought up, when not travelling further afield. I have published eight collections of poetry and a non-fiction title. *www.boomslangpoetry.blogspot.com*

SUE PROFFITT lives in Hallsands, a remote settlement situated in Start Bay, South Devon, England. Her favourite walk is from her cottage to Start Point, one of the most exposed peninsulas on the English coast, running sharply almost a mile into the sea. The lighthouse at the end of the headland has guided ships in passage along the English Channel for over 150 years, and the coastal cliffs here are the oldest in Devon. The coastline is home to many wild flowers, birds and animals. Walking the coastpath and swimming in the sea off the shingle beach always brings her home to herself. Writing poetry is central to Sue's life and is an exploration of the beauty and mystery of the more-than-human world, and of our complex human relationship with it.

OMAR SABBAGH is a widely published poet and critic. His most recent poetry collection, *Morning Lit: Portals After Alia*, was published by Cinnamon Press in 2022. A new collection of short fiction, *Y Knots*, will be published by Liquorice Fish Books this year.

JOHN SEWELL writes: When I move to a new area I identify every hill visible from the house. Then visit each summit in turn, pinpointing my house through binoculars. This two-way looking extends my personal boundaries, makes the landscape intimate and ever-present. It's easier to write love poems when you know the subject will always be there for you, no matter what.

BARRY SMITH is the director of the South Downs Poetry Festival, nurturing creative expression with writers and communities across the district. The emphasis is on placing poetry alongside other arts, including music, dance and visual art. Barry has worked as a theatre director, as a critic and as an educator. His collection *Performance Rites* draws upon his experience in facilitating the arts.

LESLIE TATE says: I'm a non-binary, Extinction Rebellion activist who interviews creative and community-engaged people weekly on radio and on my website *leslietate.com*, sometimes with a specific ecological theme. My guests frequently make the connection between mental/social health and caring for the planet. I'm engaged with the local Transition Town, Climate Café, Refill Pantry and Town/Borough Council to improve local resilience.

BONNIE THURSTON writes: I live on six acres on the side of a hill in a little valley by a creek that runs into the Ohio River. Geographically, it is both Appalachian and Ohio River Valley. Formerly a New Testament professor, I have published widely as a theologian and poet.

JAN VILLARRUBIA says: In my wild New Orleans yard, monarch butterflies lay eggs on native milkweed, hummingbirds jostle for big blue salvia and gray seeds on my bayberry attract yellow-rumped warblers. I do not wear gloves while gardening. Feeling the rich dark soil of Louisiana is meditation for me. Something of nature or spirit is found in most of my poems and plays.

GAIL WEBB was born in a mining town in Wales, lives now in Nottinghamshire. Her pamphlet, *The Thrill Of Jumping In* (Big White Shed 2021), addresses friendships, loss, ageing, the joys in life. Gail is passionate about poetry's ability to highlight the humanity in us all and to connect with others. She also writes about identities shaped by landscape and geography.

HELEN MAY WILLIAMS formerly taught at Warwick University and, as Helen May Dennis, has written extensively on twentieth-century poetry. She is also the author of *Catstrawe* (Cinnamon Press 2019) and *The Princess of Vix* (Three Drops Press 2017). Her parallel text translation of Michel Onfray's *Before Silence* is published by The High Window Press (2020). Her biographical novel, June, and her award-winning pamphlet, *Coed Cae Clear*, are also published by Cinnamon Press.

PATRICA HELEN WOOLDRIDGE has an impelling need to be outside and draws inspiration from the natural landscape, birds and the weather (especially winter). She regards walking as essential in the composition of poetry. Her publications include *Sea Poetics* (Cinnamon 2018) and *Being* (Cinnamon 2020). Her new collection *Out in the Field* won the Cinnamon Literature Award 2022. *www.poetrypf.co.uk/patriciahelenwooldridgepage.shtml*

www.ingramcontent.com/pod-product-compliance
Lightning Source LLC
Chambersburg PA
CBHW040105260626
47164CB00019B/207